Praise for
Do Unto Earth

"A must-read book for everyone who cares about the future of humanity and our planet."

—**Dr. Ervin Laszlo**, two-time Nobel Peace Prize nominee, recipient of the Goi Peace Prize and International Mandir of Peace Prize, best-selling author of Science and the Akashic Field, founder of the Laszlo Institute of New Paradigm Research and The Club of Budapest, fellow of the World Academy of Art and Science and the International Academy of Philosophy of Science

"A 911 call from Planet Earth herself, *Do Unto Earth* is a potent manifesto for living life today and forward. This book should be required reading in schools. We must act now!"

—**Mary Madeiras**, three-time Emmy-Winning director, screenwriter, Akashic Records practitioner, activist, and author

"*Do Unto Earth* is full of empowering messages and mind-bending assertions that you won't find in science or history textbooks. Given the urgent need for new solutions on this endangered planet, the ideas are worthy of further investigation."

—**Mark Gober**, author of *An End to Upside Down Thinking*, board of directors of the Institute of Noetic Sciences (IONS) and the School of Wholeness and Enlightenment (SoWE)

"From page one, I was hooked! *Do Unto Earth* merges spirituality with our environmental crisis and does it in a way that is as gripping as a blockbuster movie. Brava to Hayes, Borgens … and Pax."

—**Temple Hayes**, author, spiritual leader, animal activist, and founder of illli.org

"The channeled Spirit energy Pax states that we are at the 'crossroads of our survival' and offers us bold envisioning and direction. Mother Earth is speaking, and ancient mysteries are revealed! Let's heed and implement these game-changers for the benefit of us all."

—**Sunny Chayes**, social/human rights and environmental activist, feature writer and Chief Strategic Partner for Whole Life Times, and host of ABC's *Solutionary Sundays*

"Timely, high-level and generative wisdom detailing how we may still sustain our beautiful planet while reclaiming our collective and individual sovereignty."

—**Stephan McGuire**, director of Zürich-based NGO Cernunnos Media, Director of Tree Media Foundation

Pax and the Crossroads of Our Survival

Pax and the Crossroads of Our Survival

Volume 4 of Do Unto Earth

PENELOPE JEAN HAYES,
CAROLE SERENE BORGENS

Waterside Productions

Cover design by:
Andrew Green
Books & Illustration

Printed in the United States of America

First Printing, 2020

ISBN-13: 978-1-951805-01-2 print edition
ISBN-13: 978-1-951805-02-9 ebook edition

Waterside Productions
2055 Oxford Ave
Cardiff, CA 92007
www.waterside.com

For you—
so you know for certain that you are the change and
you have the power

Contents

Introduction xi

Volume 4 . . . . **1**
Do Unto Earth   **Pax and the Crossroads**
                    of Our Survival. 1
Chapter Ten: Planetary Energy Tumors. 3
Chapter Eleven: Earth Speaks 17
Chapter Twelve: A Crisis of Climate. 31

About the Author and Channeler. 45

Introduction

Do Unto Earth is an extraordinary conversation intended to quantum leap us forward in our spiritual evolution and journey to enlightenment. This message is not a directive delivered from a thousand feet up; this is a very personal message from and dialogue with the Divine Wisdom Source directly to you and for you. Please accept this gift with eyes clear and wide and open.

Within these pages is the blueprint for environmental repair and peace and unity on Earth, however, this booklet constitutes just one of eight volumes that together make up that blueprint. While we believe that the eight topics, as separated by these volumes, are to be understood as connected to each other and only together give the full message as intended, we also understand some readers prefer to focus on their specific areas of interest—hence these eight mini-books by volumes. (Note: Chapters within this volume are numbered as they originally appeared in the book's full-length version.)

As you begin this journey, you might like to know how this collaboration of writing began.

It is indeed my great joy and honor to communicate with the Spirit Messenger, Pax, channeled by

Carole Serene Borgens. From a young age, Carole, a former nurse, diligently studied all things metaphysical. This Spirit Messenger first visited her in the early 1990s when she was new to channeling by automatic writing. When her pen wrote the opening introduction and request for her to be a channel, she recognized the profound responsibility attached and jumped up from her office chair to pace the floor—not easy with three sleeping Irish Wolfhounds covering the carpet. Carole's initial response was to ask if she could think about it and take some time to respond, which she was given. Asking, "Why me?" Spirit responded to her: "You are new to this, you have no bad habits, and you will change none of my words." In time, Carole came to be comfortable with this blessing and so began her journey.

I, too, have been a seeker and spiritualist since my years as a teenaged runaway, and so it is a useful tool at times for me to reach out to a reputable intuitive for deeper guidance. Beginning on the fourth of February 2019, I had several long-distance Spirit channeling sessions with Carole—she was in British Columbia and I was in Florida. I had copious questions for Spirit as I sought further direction for my second title, *Do Unto Earth* (which, incidentally, is also the name of my business), while building upon the message of my first title, *The Magic of Viral Energy*. I was expanding and broadening the message of "viral energy" from personal and interpersonal goals to global concerns facing humanity and Planet Earth. I was also simultaneously establishing the Viral Energy Institute, a learning and research platform for the study of Viralenology.

Through our talks, this Spirit Messenger and I were getting to know each other and Spirit felt my passion for the plight of abused animals and species extinction, as well as my intention to bring awareness to our environmental crisis and to share the impacts of "viral energy masses"—large energetic fields created by both light and heavy intentions and action by communities, populations, industries, governments, and cultural beliefs—on Planet Earth. These disruptive energy masses create massive vibrational pockets of particular energies including love, hate, peace, discord, gratitude, violence, forgiveness, indifference, and compassion.

The Spirit Messenger seemed very interested in this direction and before long, Carole contacted me to say that Spirit wished to offer wisdom to be used by and shared through the Viral Energy Institute regarding this mission of planetary healing.

The writing began on the second of October 2019 when I sent questions to Carole who then channeled Spirit's responses by automatic writing (today, she does this via typing). It was *during* the writing that it became clear to all that this conversation would take book form and adopt the title *Do Unto Earth*.

As the answers were returned from Spirit, Carole and I both had many moments of excitement and more than a few gasps followed by, "Ooooh crikey, this is going to change everything!" The first of such revelations came in Chapter One when I asked the Spirit Messenger (whom self-identified with the moniker "**Pax**", meaning peace) to be more specific about who they are. Here was the answer...

> **"We are one with the Universe, not the Universe alone. We are the Divine Universe, yes, and the God being and the greater wisdom, that which knows and supports all and is healing, non-judgmental and tolerant, all-seeing, all-knowing, and Peace."**

Volume 4

Do Unto Earth
Pax and the Crossroads of
Our Survival

*"The climate crisis is a spiritual crisis for our entire
world. Our solutions must weave science, spirituality,
and traditional ecological knowledge with technology."*
Rose Whipple
Environmental activist from the Isanti Dakota and
Ho-Chunk Nations of American Indigenous Peoples

Chapter Ten

Planetary Energy Tumors

*P*ax, are you enjoying this conversation? I am! And, it interests me to know, do you *enjoy* experiences and the sharing of wisdom? Is enjoyment a thing for you?

We teach, we share, we collaborate, we enjoy, yes.

Do you "travel" for enjoyment? My husband and I went to Miami this past weekend to check it out, see something different, and have some fun. Do you visit other galaxies, universes, or spacetime locations for either "business" or pleasure?

We are amused by this notion. We are not in need of travel, as we exist simultaneously where thoughts take us.

Thanks for humoring me. Now, back to our "business" (which is actually a lot of fun, I think).

In my first book, prior to our talks, I mentioned a theory that I had channeled from my Higher Self consciousness about large energetic masses, or tumors, of both light and heavy *viral energy* upon the Earth that we have created and are creating by way of large pockets of love, hate, joy, fear, and all of our light and dark actions and intentions. Pax, can you validate this?

Energy tumors, well yes, Penelope, this is all over your world at this time, to the extent they can be seen from space. You need to focus on this as the world, as it is at present, is aware of heaviness and great negative change, but what to call it and how to endure or relieve it? Penelope, you have the term and the description, you now need to share the way of relief.

The heavy viral energy tumors can be seen from space!?

To be visible from space means literally the feeling of the energy radiating from those areas, not a visible-to-the eye cloud. Palpable would be another word for visible and this is the true meaning. For empaths who see and feel energy, the density of energy in those areas is palpable.

We've talked about the physical damage to our environment in that we are the cause of extreme pollution, global warming, and species

extinction, to name a few issues. May you now please speak to the *energetic* damage mankind has done to our planet, such as the byproducts of heavy energy events and actions and attitudes— energetic tumors and scars created by war, indifference, religious and cultural intolerance, hate perpetuated throughout many generations, the on-mass pain and suffering commonplace to the wholesale slaughter of animals, and the many global impacts of heavy viral energy on-scale?

These dark energies have existed always on Planet Earth. They remain in place but can be dissolved by light energy, by love and intention to raise vibration in places previously damaged. Love always prevails, and focusing love energy in or on people, places and things, animals, plants and soil, water and air, along with consistent effort to heal in those ways possible, combine to bring healing and wellness. It is the intention that makes it real.

If we put concentrated intention and light energy on these heavy energy tumors by having many people simultaneously focus their light energy on them, can we heal these pockets of heavy energy through our viral intentions?

Oh yes, this is how it is done: concentrated energy heals.

When you gather together with intention to heal—focusing energy on a specific area, group of people, energy mass, dark intentions and beliefs—and bring the healing light into focus on those targets, energy change occurs. This is palpable and this is real. Effectively moving the mass of dark energy into the light is the result.

You must also know that the epidemic of mental health dis-ease on your planet is dark energy at work. Those "sensitives" pick up, feel in all ways, dark energy and it envelops them. The descent into inability to function as a result is what must be addressed.

I believe that many forms of depression are not a "mental health crisis", meaning they are not a problem with the brain or a chemical imbalance in the brain, but rather many forms of depression are a "spiritual health crisis", meaning the depression was created by an immersion into heavy energy for a chronic period of time. Also, that to have a longstanding sense of lack of purpose can also create depression. These are energetic/spiritual crises that can be cured by energetic/spiritual therapy: Light Energy Immersion Therapy. What do you think of this as a philosophy?

Yes, this is a truth and cause for much of the mental health crisis currently experienced by your people. Sadness and emotional trauma result in dis-ease of the soul and spirit and show as depression on the quiet side and violence on the other.

Many therapies exist, the most common being drug therapy: we say this is a shortcut in the system and only masks symptoms, doing nothing to find the source so healing may begin. It is a sadness in your system that sufficient time is not allotted to the individual in need.

Natural remedies such as light therapies, as mentioned, are effective. Sunshine in an artificial form does repair emotional lows in people sensitive to seasonal change.

Removal of dark energies, family strife for example, is a beginning of the journey to wellness. It is not a quick repair; it is a slow repair, which leads to wellness.

Your First Nations peoples have the right idea in their delivering a person *back to the land to find themselves*, to find their spirit, has been their way of accepting that person's journey to wellness is managed by their extended family of support and love. They are then welcomed back into the circle.

Nature immersion—yep, when I was depressed in my youth, I could have used about three months to marinate in and equilibrate with nature. (Recently, people started calling this Forest Bathing.) What else should we know about depression and heavy/dark energy?

Those *severely* affected by dark energy are the ones responsible for crime, mass killings, and acts of violence that they may say originated with voices telling them to do so: voices in their heads. Consider this is a possession of sorts, that this energy that affects others slightly or not at all, when felt by one sensitive to it, becomes a guiding darkness, the opposite of "guiding light," in this person.

To set about moving these cells of dark energy away from your Earth atmosphere will be the beginning of healing in all ways. Those who are energy sensitive will be lifted from the grasp of what they don't know or understand but do experience negative thoughts and feelings from.

To move energy, to lighten energy, and to change the balance of energy is to bring about a change in your world in ways not previously considered related.

Yes, it is the way.

I'm inspired to help enlighten the energy on our planet and anyone with light intentions can join in this effort.

If we set about moving these cells of dark energy away from our Earth atmosphere, will the dark energy then negatively impact the space outside of our Earth's atmosphere?

The method of removing this dark energy is to neutralize it so it is away from your Earth, yes, but no other place; it is gone.

To ensure our readers are clear, is this dark energy at all the same or related in any way to what exists in space that we call Dark Energy or "dark matter" or antimatter?

You speak of anti-gravity things. What we speak of here is simply energy—human created negativity—and is readily neutralized by humans.

Let's talk further about the global viral contemplations for Planet Earth? It's one thing to gather people in large numbers to focus light energy intentions on a piece of land or a person or an event with the goal to enlighten—cleanse with light, dissolve the darkness—such as a tumor of dark energy at work, however it seems quite next-level-consciousness to *move* cells of dark energy away from our Earth atmosphere. (I envision our comic book character Superman mightily flying upwards from Earth and into the outer planetary atmosphere while carrying a gigantic ball of dark energy.) How do we accomplish moving cells of dark viral energy away from our atmosphere?

Creative Visualization is a process by which attention is focused on an area or thing and intention placed with it. In this case, the mass focus on an area covered with dark energy, with the intention of neutralizing, dispelling, eliminating, vaporizing that energy—while *visualizing* it being there, then beginning to clear, then completely clearing—holds the power to do so. You may dissolve a cloud using this method—try it.

Ah, yes, you mentioned this before and so this past weekend, while lying on the beach, I tried to

dissolve a cloud using my thought power and it worked! Part of me was not surprised because you told me it would work, and the other part of me was like—*holy cow, I just dissolved that cloud!*

We mere earthlings are not used to thinking this way; that our thought power can move or affect something in the physical world. And yet, it worked.

You have my attention, Pax. How does it work?

Intention, pure and simple. It is the placing of intention behind a thought.

We discussed this earlier and you have put it into practice.

As we have previously stated, the use of intention with thought is responsible for great things, from building pyramids to curing one's own dis-ease. This is well known in your Earth time and practiced by those who trust.

This is going to be vital in healing our world, I can tell. I'd like to keep going in a lesson in creative visualization and conscious creation. You've told us, "When the student is ready the teacher appears." Well, I'm here to learn. May you please give me a next step or assignment beyond dissolving a cloud?

Dissolving clouds tests only your belief in self. The use of this creative visualization extends to all needs on your planet. Consider creating wellness from dis-ease and consider creating peace from its opposite—all things are possible when your intention is placed where need exists; you speak your intention and see and feel the result. It is *your belief in the result* and *the visualization of the result* and the *feeling of having and being the result* that is the exercise.

We share the how and you decide the why and what.

This is indeed very empowering. Although, if we found it as easy as this sounds, we'd all be manifesting our "whats". Many people have heard and read about these methods and there have been a few popular movie documentaries that promote the concept of which you describe. What else do we need to know in order to learn conscious creation and visualization for manifestation?

That people have not learned the earlier lesson means only they have not chosen to learn. We say that to look to the above, again, for explanation may be useful: all things are possible when your intention is placed where need exists, you speak your intention, and see and feel the result. It is *your belief in the result* and *the visualization of the result* and the *feeling of having and being the result* that is the exercise.

There are many books on visualization, attraction, manifestation, affirmations, and conscious creation. There's even a book, originally

published in 1978, with the exact title *Creative Visualization* by Shakti Gawain. It was a pop-culture phenomenon at the time. (At least it was in some areas and with some audiences.)

We've had a lot of time to incorporate these lessons and to become a more empowered people, yet it's still not mainstream thinking or practice.

In my viral energy work I recommend the concentration of thought-energy to heal people and disruptions in nature. I have a colleague who did some light energy work in Japan to heal a man's land where nothing was growing and the animals were dying. She led a group who encircled the water well at the center of the negative energy; it worked, and the land was healed. Incidentally, this friend is of the opinion that Egypt and New Zealand are also in need of energy healing for various reasons.

What land or pieces of land do you see as sick or in need of energy healing?

Your Mother Earth is in distress globally. The choices of New Zealand and Egypt are interesting.

My colleague visited New Zealand and while it's a land and people of extraordinary beauty, she witnessed that too many people are hooked on the drug fentanyl. She felt it as a place in need of healing.

We suggest the basis for these choices is underwhelming and a deeper introspection may find evidence of a need throughout the Middle East. Generations of doom-filled regimes have led to endless dis-ease in that area as there is no growth or refreshing of energy in place. Distrust and hatred and greed and warring have contributed and now it is time to bring the greater good to the area. Separation of cultures has been the way and in order to heal, there needs to be inclusion. To send out healing energy here and as chosen, New Zealand, is a good beginning. What you will find in the former far outweighs the latter, however. For a variety of reasons, there is need globally, some regions more deeply than others, so you may systematically circle the globe focusing on specific regions as you go.

To heal from greed and hate and intolerance and racism and discrimination is a goal.

You will be supported by the Universe in this.

The Middle East—yes, this makes sense to me and is a great place to begin.

Another friend, who is an intuitive, said that she feels a palpable repelling force from Egypt-energy. Yet, I know other people who are stimulated by the energy of Egypt and experience it as very enlightening and attractive. Is there one particular energy indeed present around Egypt? Also, is there undiscovered ancient wisdom at Giza, such that we would benefit to focus on uncovering it and then learn from ancient people's wisdom found there?

Ancient wisdom is found in many forms, and some energy is dark energy. Any civilization of that age will be imbued with good and evil, light and dark, and uncovering artifacts from those early times will have all these attached. It is for the archaeologists who know this fact to protect themselves and work areas while uncovering past mysteries. There are baffling happenings surrounding those who do this work in certain ancient sites, and no other explanations exist for the negative energies and fates that befell some workers. It is the way of it.

How will the Universe support the work to heal the world by way of concentrated healing energy intention? (I have to say, it gives me goosebumps to hear you say that the Universe will support me.)

The Universe will support by bringing to our writings the masses of people looking for guidance in how their thoughts and intentions can result in Earth healing. They need to gather together and have a leader who will create the format for mass healing gatherings.

As your media formats are established, they will touch people around the globe and result in a critical mass creation, the power of which is unmistakable. It is the logical next step from your first book and the Viral Energy Institute and then our collaboration and sharing of purpose with this following. It is mystical and magical and a place of peace and purpose for the many.

This makes me very happy. How do you envision or see these "en mass healing gatherings"? Will we do this in person in venues like sports stadiums, or will we connect with people through television and radio broadcasts, and online through cyberspace?

Initially, these gatherings are through your cyberspace as it is getting the most with the least effort, the least upheaval for people, and the communication this way leads to splinter groups in person as time goes on.

The magic of television is to be considered, as this becomes a splinter group as target markets are considered in order of preference. There needs to be connection of the most numbers in the soonest time, so this combination is to be considered.

Consider it considered.
Going back to the cyberspace gatherings and in-person gatherings, I feel like the Universe is already working to get this project rolling. I met a very talented singer, a vocal artist from France, Erin Kann, who creates beautiful tracks of music and vocals that act like medicine to repair body organs and disease by way of healing sound vibration. She calls them Sound Balms. We have collaborated on a custom Sound Balm titled *Earth's*

Voice as the track for a guided meditation—Global Viral Contemplation—to heal Mother Earth and to aid people all over the world in accessing their Higher Self wisdom. Erin has worked with a bio-energetician and an astrophysicist to verify her methods of healing and enlightenment through sound vibration.

Do you see merit in this project—healing sound vibration in focused energy intention work for Mother Earth?

Of course, this is to be.

The ancients knew sound energy and its uses in healing (as well as warring at times: certain frequencies can make people quite crazy if used for extended times and can shatter glass).

Some frequencies are healing and enhance meditation—the Om vibration and sound as example. Sound therapy and in your current place, music therapy, which is a derivation, works miracles in certain applications. This is yet another tool to use in the healing process.

You must know that playing sounds of musical notes and vibrations increases plant growth, crop yields, soothes people and animals, and brings peace where heard.

Chapter Eleven
Earth Speaks

I've read that Earth has a magical energy grid and that energies run through ley lines around the globe—straight lines drawn between various historic structures—and that these ley lines were recognized by ancient ancestors to provide energy for enlightenment. I've been to two places that are said to be ley line vortexes: Mount Shasta in California, and Sedona, Arizona (there are four vortexes in Sedona: Airport Mesa, Cathedral Rock, Bell Rock, and Boynton Canyon), and yes indeed, I felt a powerful vibration. While I won't share an exhaustive list, some other ley lines or ley line vortexes that I've heard about are: the Great Pyramids of Giza, the Stonehenge Circle, the Great Wall of China, the Nusa Islands, the southern tip of South Africa, the tower of Glastonbury Tor in England, Es Vedrà on the Spanish island of Ibiza, Chichén Itzá on Mexico's Yucatán Peninsula, Mexico's Mayan ruins in Tulum, Maui's Haleakalā volcano, and of course there must be more. Are these ley

lines a real thing, and if so, may you please explain what they are?

It is the case that ley lines are found encircling the globe, your Mother Earth globe, and as they intersect there are power centers where the believers congregate for healing. Many experience great change and many experience great insights, and all experience something whether recognized at the time or later, but the experience is enlightening in different ways. Higher consciousness is achieved and clear thinking and feeling and visions are a result of spending time near a vortex. For some, the power is too great and physical feelings of unwellness occur—for these sensitives it is a need to distance somewhat from the power center. Those lesser developed on their spiritual path may feel little until the cumulative effect is noticed.

The power is there for the enlightened.

We are here to say these are indeed the places where mankind should be concentrating energy. It is at these sites that collective consciousness and personal consciousness can be greatly impacted for the better. The positive energy at these sites has been gathering for centuries and can't help but affect pilgrims who visit there.

Well, this is intriguing. How should we be utilizing these powerful ley lines?

The awakening of the mind to the potential for change is the first step. Understanding the details and understanding the power is next. Respect for these places must be present in the hearts and minds of visitors. Change will occur when in the presence of the energies.

Ley lines do exist with all their potential to positively affect those in their presence. Make the trek and find out.

In times of old, Earth's peoples knew of these places and traveled on pilgrimages to be healed and changed in many ways. The idea that they need only visit and believe was appealing, and it is the case.

Today there are believers and non-believers, but the fact remains that those who visit these areas are changed. On the inside is the movement of the water in the body—it is the gravitational pull that makes the difference. See it for yourself.

My dear, Pax, I'm going to have to ask you to please expand on this: "On the inside is the movement of the water in the body—it is the gravitational pull that makes the difference." I get the gravitation pull on water idea; it's like the power of the full moon and other astrological phenomenon. What I need help with is *why* this movement of the water of our body composition affects our inner-power-charge, empowerment, healing, and enlightenment?

It is empowering in its awareness of self and Self being increased and energy being catapulted to the highest levels known to a person. It parts the clouds so that truth and possibilities are brought forward to the knowing. Infinite possibilities are seen, and the mind is opened to life's next steps. The journey becomes clear.

When in these power centers, all life opens to view, and each person's experience differs but is the same in that a shift takes place in personal energy.

I would then say that Mother Earth is interactive with us, she shares her energy with us, she's a living energetic organism and she speaks to us in many ways.

Does Earth have emotions? Does Earth cry or mourn for her sickness and diseases? Does Earth speak to us somehow: in the wind, in whispers?

Well yes, all of this you suggest is the case. And Mother Earth has emotions and currently begins to show them in not the subtle ways of past. Where She has whimpered and cried in past, your Mother speaks now in floods and fires and eruptions and earth shifts and typhoons, tornadoes, and hurricanes.

If you can think of this, the anger pockets in place around the globe, those black spots of dark energy, they transmit to your Earth people with sensitivities and the need to punish, showing themselves in mass killings and acts of violence of all types.

Is this, too, the manifestation of pockets of "viral energy"—large tumors of contagious energy?

It is a contagious *viral energy* mass of punishment taken up by those who think they can cure all by violence. Being infected with this dark energy fuels their need for validation and they escalate to what you see in your world today.

Here's what I've discovered through years of viral energy work: It is through our dark intentions and actions that we create the dark energy, and then the dark energy creates more dark (negative and heavy) energy and actions. (Or light energy creates more light energy, of course.) And, this occurs through a viral movement of energy— both light or dark energy are contagious and also transfer passively, by osmosis, simply through immersion in and around such dark energy.

Is this all correct?

Indeed.

Dark energy is of your people's creation and grows as it is taken on by people sensitive to it, resulting in negative acts which perpetuate the cycle: more is created, and more is held in your space and time. Wholesale healing is needed—intention to clear this energy can be undertaken by people alone, or in groups around the globe. To pray for peace and pray for healing energy to replace dark energy is the way.

It seems that worldwide there's been a higher frequency of mega-sized storms, fires, tsunamis, and earthquakes.

Consider the arrival of fire and tornado. Consider the almost constant pummeling of Planet Earth now by natural disaster. Is this not a warning; a heads-up to your population at this time that enough is enough, and acts must be cleaned up and new ways of thinking begun and acted upon? This is the intention. How it is received determines your future. Your peaceful forward motion in time is dependent on decisions made by your people and your leaders now.

The places most affected are somewhat peaceful locations; places that appear to hold more light energy vibration than heavy energy vibration. Of course, appearances might be deceiving. Are the locations of the Mother-Earth-Speaks natural cataclysms the same locations where our greed and violence and other dark actions have created masses of dark energy? Or, do the eruptions show up in non-dark-energy related geographical locations because these places have vulnerabilities or weaknesses, or is there another reason?

That these vulnerable areas of Earth continue to be troubled by natural disasters is a combination of reasons. Mother Earth has been damaged and hurts, resources have not been well managed to the extent the area is vulnerable, and what happens underground is also causal—fault lines being one.

Some might say that ravaging the places of people showing great wealth and great narcissism and great self-interest sends a message. Contrasting that is the damage to people who do not fit this description: it is Mother Nature stating it is time to move off this land. Your Earth has been badly treated and this can go on only so long before Mother Nature shows you the way to her regained wellness.

Those who rise from the ashes will continue to do so, claiming the land over the constant reminders that natural disaster continues, sometimes annually, and what does it take for the message to be heard?

It is also to be considered that the First Nations peoples of old, very long ago in your time, *when removed from their lands sometimes left an energy field around it* that led to it not being inhabited by others for long periods as unfriendly experiences such as nature would show, were too often experienced. Is this the case in California? Is this the case when Moana Kea erupts, and her sacred self is shaking? Is it?

I say you are giving us a rhetorical question and that it is in fact the case in California and the Moana Kea volcano in Hawaii.

Should we leave these energy fields in place until First Nations people are returned there or they themselves lift it, or should we all work on the energy to turn it into energy that is more hospitable for life in these places?

Oh, now this is a question. Would you decide it right to override the actions and beliefs of those who consider these sacred lands? If there were to be an en mass healing and shifting of energy, it would best be undertaken with the blessing and participation of those who placed that energy for their purposes and beliefs. To go against those beliefs, albeit with good intentions, would add to the burden on that land.

Knowing this, I would only wish to undergo a mass healing *with* the blessing and leadership and guidance of the peoples who placed that energy there.

Do the present-day descendants of those peoples know of these intentionally placed energies?

Oh yes, and it would be considered their traditional territory and protected as best they can from the encroachment of tourism and those who would take from the land without respect. This is not a good thing to do.

Old energies remain in place and are to be considered and respected.

Understood. Maybe one day these energy fields will be lifted, *if* that's what those First Nations peoples decide. Although, it sounds like these energies are still needed to protect the land from those who still haven't the heart and mind to care for it with respect and love.

When we were talking about the ways of the First Nations peoples, we had a discussion about the Dakota Pipeline in America and the effects on the Standing Rock Sioux Tribe. Here's a thought:

could the Sioux Nation place such an energy field around their sacred land, thereby deterring the success of the Dakota Pipeline (an energetic kink in the pipe, so to speak)?

Indeed, this could be, however, to be destructive would not be a positive step. It is the way of this to educate the invaders in history and tradition and try to work together in respect and harmony. While this is a lofty goal, efforts continue to enforce what rights the Sioux have while bringing awareness to the world of the bigger picture—the protection of sacred land so as to not injure themselves emotionally or anger ancestral spirits.

In Brazil, tremendous chunks of rainforest have been cleared to create space for oil palms. Also, in Indonesia, the harvesting of palm oil is damaging the rainforests and decimating wildlife including orangutans. When tallied back in 2017, over fifty thousand orangutans on the islands of Borneo and Sumatra had died because of palm oil deforestation. It's heartbreaking and unacceptable, yet it's accepted. Do you know, Pax, how many of our products contain palm oil? These include food products, candy and snacks, cosmetics, biofuel, animal feed, pharmaceuticals, and industrial-use items. We are mowing down forests so that corporations can take this natural resource. How can we protect the indigenous animals and natural habitats and ecosystems?

Despite your outrage at the ramifications of growing and harvesting this crop, it is a dietary staple.

And so, what's the solution?

We suggest the humanitarian aspect of this be taken to the governments of the countries involved, along with an alternative offered in harvesting methods and buffer zones left for animal population solace and survival.

What can you tell us about the great Amazon rainforest burning? Are forest fires set on purpose to clear land to raise more cows for export commerce? Let's narrow in on the big one of recent times: were the very destructive Amazon fires in 2019 set on purpose?

This is an extreme example and not to be repeated, but fires are often set in the Amazon rain forest by farmers—to create grazing land is a need for some. Fortunately, the growth there is so rapid that the jungle can take over cleared areas in short time and reforestation is managed. The area is habitat for many animals and also growing area for cattle and crops. They exist in harmony, usually.

To pray for return to health of this Amazon rain forest is helpful.

How critical to Planet Earth's health is the Amazon?

The rain forest is critical to the health of the planet as it is responsible for cleaning the air to a very large percentage.

Let's talk about the bush fires in Australia that are devastating wildlife. What is the cause of these historic fires and why are seasonal bush fires worse than ever?

Some fires are man-made, and these are no different.

Agricultural farmers versus sheep farmers, always contradiction in rationale and need for land use.

Some who clear land for planting do so with controlled burning which can become out of control.

The climate, high temperatures in Australia have been relatively constant, but even they grow more intense in this time.

Pax, I'd like to follow up on what you said: "Agricultural farmers versus sheep farmers, always contradiction in rationale and need for land use."

How does this contradiction between crop farmers and sheep farmers relate to the cause of these fires? Have some fires been deliberately set in some sort of a battle of the farmers, or to sabotage the other? I'm trying to figure out the connection between these two types of farmers to the fires.

When the indigenous people clear land for farming and to keep firebreaks in place, they do so by controlled burns. There can be accidents when due to wind and weather a fire becomes larger than intended—there would be no intentional damage to the Earth created in the name of protection and prevention.

When non-indigenous farmers do the same, the results can be expected to be similar. The sheep take growth down to the dirt, which is not appreciated by the agricultural farmers, and the sheep farmers continue to need grazing land for their flocks and there is a push and pull ongoing. Neither would knowingly harm the land so that it could not recover. This would be disputed by some, but those who need healthy land to support livestock and crops are wise in the ways of conservation.

Fires in Australia occur each year during their hottest months. During the 2020 fire season, the fires covered six times the land and forests of what was burned by the 2019 Amazonia fires. More than half a billion animals perished in the 2020 fires in Australia, and many experts say the number is much higher. The loss of thousands of koalas has been called "a national tragedy" by the Australian government. It seems that there is a growing link between climate change/rising temperatures and why these fires rage on no matter what initially sparked them.

Pax, what do we need to know about Australia and these bush fires?

This is not the way of the ancients in this place, as they managed control of their soil and bush over their time of existence. They see the future of this now and are deeply saddened by man's inability to manage the resources.

If these fires go into the ground and find the coal, it will spell even greater disaster and that, over time, results in the inability of that portion of Earth to support life.

OMG—the coal!

Australia is the world's largest exporter of both coal and natural gas. The ground is rich with coal and the mines that bring coal to the surface are concentrated in about the very same places as the fires; no one is talking about the potential for the fires to reach the coal supplies.

We need to sound the alarm.

It is a crossroads now for this continent; a place of determining future, or not, for healthy life on that soil. Desecration is the present situation. How repair is managed determines habitability in future.

I wonder if we can call in outside help. Is there anything our interstellar visitors could do to help?

We say that the way of this connection is to not interfere in what mankind—the Earth inhabitants—have created. What could be remains unknown and what will be, the same.

In times past the people would gather and pray for rain. Now your people don't understand that they have the capability to set their intention to this, people around the globe, and by the power of their intention and prayer, bring healing moisture to this suffering region. It is so simple and so not practiced—the power of intention and prayer together make mountains move.

Let us all pray prayers of thanks and gratitude, send up light thoughts and pure intentions and visualize rain quenching fires. May people around the globe unite in prayer and thought intention for the continent of Australia, and for peace in the world, healing for people in peril, and protection for animals in crisis. Let's send thoughts of love and peace to people and wildlife and farmed animals.

We are here to say that the next generation of your Earth people bring change and repair and higher vibration to your Earth—there is hope. Now is time for those in power to listen to the youth as their idealistic and pure intentions and guidance pave the way to this growth. Trust in this.

Chapter Twelve
A Crisis of Climate

When we were discussing mysteries of the Earth, you said something that I now want to go back to because your words bring up the exact argument made by climate change deniers. We were talking about sunken civilizations and you said, "If you ask about remains of previous civilizations, then yes, very much, as over time the seas have risen and coastal inhabitants and villages have been taken by the tides. It is a repeating event now on your planet as the seas again rise and those nearby are and will be impacted by loss of land and lifestyle. History repeats itself in climate change, ice ages come and go, warming and cooling cycles, and life goes on."

And so, those who say that anthropogenic global warming is a hoax or fabrication will say that you are making their point. I know numerous people who think this way. Just yesterday, I had conversations with two separate individuals about the environment (the environment is "trending", top-of-mind, and all the rage—literally) and both of them said that they don't believe in manmade climate change. To say that I felt frustrated is an understatement. I held back my reaction and instead asked them *why* they don't believe it.

In a nutshell: they believe the Earth merely goes through natural cycles. You have confirmed these natural cycles.

Science can show the statistics of this.

Okay, let's look at the statistics.

In the United States, the National Aeronautics and Space Administration (NASA) says that climate change is extremely likely and is "greater than ninety-five percent probability" to be the result of human activity. Their data shows measurements of atmospheric carbon dioxide from ice-core samples that date back eight hundred thousand years ago. To see a line chart of climate over these many thousands of years, it looks like numerous evenly sized waves and then, starting in 1950, a tsunami with its crest not yet realized.

The Intergovernmental Panel on Climate Change (IPCC) could not be more clear that we are sitting far above pre-industrial levels and that this is human-induced warming, which correlates to the Industrial Age: cars, factories, grossly scaled meat production, deforestation, and other factors of human pollution—all elevating greenhouse gas emissions.

Planet Earth has cycled through warming and cooling over the millennia and what you experience today is not a natural cycle. It is a speeded-up version and a deepening of severity version and a possibly irreversible version of what has gone before, certainly from the standpoint of continued human habitation. It is what it is.

Your science has documented ice ages and their beginnings and endings, warmings that followed, and the repeat—this now is at a level of severity never before experienced by your Earth.

However, many people still don't believe the latest data. What do you know that even our data doesn't that might prove to climate naysayers that global warming of today is caused by humans and not just natural cycles of the Earth?

For anyone to see the fouling done by your industry of air and water, soil and all things growing as a result, and attempt to deny the correlation, shows them to have heads firmly embedded in sand—a pity and a travesty and you know who you are.

Until awareness comes, Earth continues to foul and your people will go—"to where?"—they will be first to ask. Theirs will be the last seats on the bus to forgiveness and safety.

Could an asteroid collision cause an ice age and/or major climate change on Earth, as many believe? Has this ever been the case?

It could and it has and could once again. It is the beginning and the end of what is and what will be. Cataclysmic it is and not in your immediate future.

To be crystal clear, are humans creating our present-time crisis of climate?

You are doing so, yes, and it is always humans creating and recreating, destroying and recovering. Retaining status quo all-is-well would be a consideration, yes?

Your people's continued focus on self and not Earth is responsible. You know this and steps are being taken by some to change. Too little too late has been the case in past; do not let it be so now.

And, is anthropogenic global warming a real and imminent threat to human survival on Earth?

Well, yes, and it is known to your leaders as well as your people. We have discussed the ways forward toward solution. Get on it, people, please.

On behalf of your Mother Earth and all who rely on her, we ask for action.

For those who believe in Earth's cyclical nature but do not believe that we are in a new era of anomaly that is far out of balance to the former natural cycles, for those who do not believe that this major blip in the data is directly tied

to industrial age human pollution—what message do you have for them?

Wake up and smell the pollution in your air. Go to the ocean or river and drink the water—go ahead. Do you find clean and pure or do you simply reject the idea of drinking from your oceans and rivers? Look at the soils in your agricultural areas and see pollution there from chemicals plus polluted air and water—how do you feel about your food growing there?

It is a case of opening the mind to reality; of seeing what is.

I'd like to ask you about the city of Venice, Italy which was not long ago affected by high water that hit seventy-four inches; the highest flood water in fifty years. However, even greater water levels were recorded in Venice in 1966. So, what was the cause of the high water back then?

Tidal action being affected by moon activity combined with severity and length of rains all play a role—many natural sources touch results such as this—there will be more and all are somewhat different in their origin, but the result looks the same: flooding, high water to levels unprecedented.

Some people say that they know we are polluting the Earth in a terrible way, and yet they still believe that we're only partly responsible for

climate change. They also believe that the Earth may have had past natural events such as volcanic eruptions that caused the greenhouse effect and we are just contributing a small amount. What would you say to those who say, "I don't believe that we 100% created climate change,"? Let's be as clear and strong worded as possible. These people don't believe the data. What can you tell them to prove it?

Let us not spend time attempting to prove to closed minds what they don't wish to believe. Let us, instead, address the partial responsibility they agree to and begin there to clean their way of living to reduce pollution in their own lifestyles.

That they agree to some damage; let them agree to some level of fixing and repair of what has been done. This should be a place to begin with all who take some little responsibility, or large portion— do your best, each of you, to repair the damage you see.

Of course, you don't need to read our latest IPCC reports, yet how do you know that we have a global warming crisis? Pax, how does the Spirit World sense and detect an out-of-norm and unnatural rise in our global temperature?

We are not a gauge of temperature; we are a gauge of what is, in the overall on your Planet Earth. That your reporting of fear and requests for assistance in diagnosing and repairing Earth damage comes to us through thoughts and prayers is our entry into the overall knowing of your presence in this time and place of fear and not understanding the way forward, as it is with all things.

So, when we send up prayers, they come to you? May you please share how it works when we send up prayers and they are received by the Spirit World?

As the heaviness of energy and emotional unwellness on your Planet Earth impacts your people and your environment, it is known to Spirit and felt.

When people pray using the name of a deity or divine one, you still know and feel their prayer?

That you do not pray to us does not result in our inability to feel the energy coming up from your people. Some pray to deities and some pray to Mother Earth and many saints and protectors of civilizations past and present—the energies transmit like ripples on a pond and are felt far and wide. There is an awareness and as we are included in the requests for healing and sharing of solutions, we become a part of the team as it were.

And what does the Spirit World team have to say about the state of our environment?

Moving ahead in time we see your world glowing—this is not in health but in excess heat. Now is the time to take steps to stop global warming.

Your world is in for a crisis of greater proportion than is now believed. It is a crisis of climate and rising waters. Too soon there will be a realization that the time is now, the time of it being too late to fix. In some geographic areas that is the case. In others on higher ground change comes to ensure life goes on, but it is still ignoring the underlying cause.

Industry money has been known to support politicians who then assist in lowering standards for industrial waste and contamination regulation. This game must not continue. It is for these kingpins of government and industry to know they are using the global population as a pawn in their game.

Who are the "kingpins of government and industry" to which you refer?

Industry and political leaders, CEOs, bankers and those who control the federal reserves, for example—the top 1% who rule all through allocation of and receipt of $$$.

How do you allow so few to control so many for so little in return? This is a travesty and must stop. Where is the social conscience of the many? Standing up and being heard is the only way to begin the end to this practice. Unite and make the difference in your world.

We wish to speak of the change in the minds of your people as being the need, and we wish to speak of the change in structure of your governments also being a need. We speak of how and when and why.

The time is now to advance the movement of love throughout your planet. The power of love is what will move you through from decline to ascent in all ways.

How does one clear-cut a forest when one loves the trees and the animals who make them their home? How does one overfish the oceans when one loves the purity and cleanliness of the waters and the life it holds? How does one treat the planet as a garbage dump when one loves the earth and the grasses and the flowers? And how does one allow for pollution to the degree you experience, when one loves the freshness and purity of the air and the birds who fly in it?

Renew and recharge and replace the man-made pollutants with the purity of the planet as it was created.

It is in your hands now. We charge you with the responsibility of cleaning up your own mess. Only your generation, and we repeat, Only Your Generation, can make this difference. To wait longer is to step over the threshold into the place of non-return, non-sustainable, and non-renewable. Can you live with that?

No, Pax, we can't.

Please imagine that you are looking into the eyes of the most powerful leaders on this planet today (those individuals who have the ability to change policies)—what would you say directly to them?

You have the floor.

Without integrity and true belief in change and the relaxation of need for supreme power and the motivation of greed among your leaders, no healing of your planet is to be.

We wish to speak of this need and the way forward to achieve it. To go forward without regard for natural resources is to sign the death warrant for the planet. Harmony comes easily when greed is left out of the equation. Do you understand this? It is greed that motivates and causes acquisitions to be of key importance. When those acquisitions involve taking liberties, rights, land, from others, it is not appropriate, healthy, or cause for celebration. It should be seen as bullying from great heights when carried out by countries, gangs, and big business. Step aside from these human conditions and look toward the elevation of consciousness and actions. It is time.

It is our message to your time that the end is near for your Earth. Go forward in the knowledge that as you sow, so shall you reap.

Mankind is not listening to the signals in nature.

Ours is the purpose and ours is the intention to put forward the truth and the lessons from galactic history that will bring heightened awareness and resolve to bring peaceful change to your Mother Earth.

What would you like to say directly to our people?

The future of your planet is in the hands of the children and the elders, and that fusion creates the answers. This fusion is beginning now, but it is to be publicized and pushed and palpated and postulated and practiced. It is to be recognized and, rather like the dunes, looked over to see what is behind it and in front of it, and we say that equals energy. That is the energy of the old and wise coupled with the energy of the young and idealistic; a wonderful combination. As tribal elders sit in circle and speak their recollections and ensure their oral and written traditions and histories do not disappear, this shall be the way of the current elders of civilizations, countries, regions, business, etc., so that each area of expertise is covered and there is someone there to accept their knowledge for the purpose of storing and cataloging and sharing.

It is to be recognized that the true worth of a person is what they will give, and now we ask for the giving of time and energy, interest and talent to protect that which will take your people into their next pathway, that of going back to the future or going forward into the past.

Much like our signature which is the sign of infinity, this is the path to take—forward becomes backward becomes forward again. Past, present and future all in one, this is the secret and this is your path.

It is the reliving of the old wisdom and the relearning of the new—yes relearning. Nothing new is ever new—it is a repeat of past wisdom that has been left out and forgotten. There is no new information. *When discoveries are made you may consider that they were in use in other planetary systems before Earth was a player.* Yes, this is the truth: someone has done it before and thousands of years ago as well. So, when your intellect sprouts wings and flies into the realm of what you thought not possible or even imagined, wrong; it was and is and will be again. Yours is to resurrect the old and call it new. But we know the reality.

While the world takes a few more turns, we wish to say that actions speak louder than words. To this end we wish to inform that the best truly is to be for your society. There will be change and growth and making the best of each day and planning for world peace becomes at the forefront. This comes about through change in national leadership and quiet and strong revolution among the people to the end that no sub-standard leadership will be tolerated. This begins now and grows to mammoth proportions resulting in leadership moving from corruption to clean and clear thinking and acting for the common good.

We ask for all mankind to adopt the ways of the aboriginal peoples whose stewardship of their land kept it for all their generations in the condition of pristine wilderness. This is a beginning for the next phase of your history that will show the intention toward wellness for all. Practicing this brings wellness to all, to the globe, to your resources and environments, and begins the healing you know is needed. It will be your resurrection from the current path of low actions to the higher good being sought and achieved. This becomes a bright star in your people's evolution.

Vibration of the planet will change with the collective consciousness of the people, of course, and why do you think otherwise? Your world is impacted greatly by the thoughts you put out there, as are your bodies and minds and the plants and animals. What you think, you radiate, and what you radiate, you are. That simple. We are here to ask the people of your world to look within. What you see there is a microcosm of what you experience outside of your self. Think on that and correct it.

Yes, we are here to say the time is now to be aware of what you each can do, in your way, to halt the progress of decimation of your planet. Do not think each of you is powerless against tyranny and against developers, and against tree-cutters, and all that comes your way to interfere with the continued well-being of your race and planet. Light always wins over darkness.

Each person is imbued with power—more than is often thought. As individuals, you have power and as groups of individuals, even greater. It is for you to understand that banding together for the common good is what will make the difference.

The best of the best are working to save your world—why not become one of them and make your own contribution.

Change is coming as quickly as you can make it.

· ·● ∞ ●· ·

About the Author and Channeler

*P*enelope Jean Hayes is a new consciousness author, television personality, and speaker. She has appeared on-camera hundreds of times as an expert guest on programs including *Dr. Phil*, *ABC News*, as well as international news specials and telecasts. She is the foremost leader in the field of contagious and osmotic energy known as Viralenology, founder of the Viral Energy Institute, and author of the book *The Magic of Viral Energy: An Ancient Key to Happiness, Empowerment, and Purpose*.

Carole Serene Borgens channels Pax, the Divine Wisdom Source. Carole is a former nurse and longtime student of metaphysics. She has been channeling Spirit since the early 1990s when she was chosen by Pax and given the title "Spirit Messenger". Carole continues to write and provide in-person and remote sessions for clients around the globe, and she refers to her gift of channeling as "the greatest blessing in my life."

Of this trio, Pax says, "A good team we three."

www.PaxWisdom.com
www.PenelopeJeanHayes.com
www.CaroleSereneBorgens.com

www.ingramcontent.com/pod-product-compliance
Lightning Source LLC
Chambersburg PA
CBHW022132280326
41933CB00007B/659